37 Killer Tricks to Get a Job Anywhere

Jesús Marrone

37 Killer Tricks to Get a Job Anywhere

First edition:
December 2024.
Copyright © Jesús Marrone (JesusMarrone.com).

Proofreading:
ChatGPT.

Front and back cover design:
Luis Carneiro (LuisCarneiro.es), with the help of Firefly AI.

All rights reserved:
Partial reproduction is permitted if it is of a small excerpt from the book, provided that the title and author are acknowledged.
Reproduction beyond the above requires the express permission of the author.

To Cronos, *the figure in Greek mythology who represents time, and to the company of the same name that trusted me to work as a Technical Writer in English.*

INDEX

INTRODUCTION

DISCLAIMER

PERFORMANCE

1. Be persistent and don't give up
2. Be productive
3. Invest your first hour of the day in job searching
4. Consider working for lower-skilled positions as an investment for the future

SKILLS

5. Learn languages
6. Learn industry-relevant programs
7. Learn keyboard shortcuts for efficiency

NETWORKING

8. Inform your contacts about your career goals
9. Attend events to expand your network
10. Join or create groups to connect with people

LINKEDIN

11. Create a complete profile
12. Set your profile to #OpenToWork?
13. Master the search tools
14. Save your job alerts
15. Search for job postings
16. Discover vacancies before the position is published
17. Connect with people and network with them
18. Ask for referrals

CHATGPT

19. CV ideas
20. Cover letter creation
21. Interview practice
22. Salary Research
23. Job Search Assistance

WEBSITES

24. Create alerts on Google
25. Search for companies, recruiters and job boards
26. Spontaneous applications
27. Search in different languages

CV

28. Highlight the city, position, experience, results, skills, and languages
29. One CV template for each position
30. Rename your CV file to include your name and the position

INTERVIEWS

31. Increase your chances of landing interviews
32. Word document for interview plan
33. Before the interview
34. During the interview
35. After the interview

ORGANIZE YOUR JOB SEARCH MATERIALS ONLINE

36. Save all your job-search materials
37. Keep a record of all your applications

ACKNOWLEDGMENTS

INTRODUCTION

When I was a kid in the 80s, my father told me that Computer Science and English would be the future. My parents enrolled my brother and me in private English classes, and for Christmas, we received an Amstrad CPC.

As a Spanish native, I never thought I could work outside my country, especially since I am a copywriter. I assumed they would prefer a native English speaker. Nevertheless, I kept improving my language skills and learning new technology tools.

In 2022, while living in Madrid with my wife, she told me she had found a great job in Luxembourg. We decided to move there since I could work remotely, but I told her it would be very difficult for me to find a job.

Still, I began sending out CVs, exploring different positions, learning French, reading books about finding a job, and brainstorming new strategies. I was frustrated but continued pushing forward. And when we were considering returning to Spain, I finally found the job!

Based on my experience, I've decided to compile all the strategies I used, to help others in their job search. I hope these tips will help you too!

Jesús Marrone

DISCLAIMER

Please note that this book offers general advice, so maybe some of them don't fit your situation now. Just take them into consideration and try whatever you feel like is going to get you a job.

This book has been written in English, so the tips provided are based on this language. **Just adapt the tricks to the language you are applying for.** But just note that more and more people are mixing languages.

For example:

- You might see a job posting written in English, but requiring someone who speaks Spanish.

- You might find a job posting written in French, but looking for an English speaker.

So try to search both in your language and in other relevant languages, such as English.

PERFORMANCE

1.- Be persistent and don't give up

Getting a job is always frustrating. We all have suffered the same situations: sending hundreds of CVs to get a few responses, making interviews and then they disappear… That happens everywhere, so don't be shocked.

Your job now is to search for a job. Your aim is not to find a job, your aim is to search for a job. Why? To not get frustrated. Getting a job doesn't depend on you; it depends on someone else. So never put a goal that depends on another person, put a goal that depends only on you. Your aim is to search for a job, that's it.

Never give up. Keep being persistent in your job search; don't stop. Find ways to stay motivated, even when facing your 234th refusal. Prepare yourself for rejection with most CVs you send, and celebrate with a beer when they ask you for an interview.

2.- Be productive

Type faster. You are going to spend a lot of time writing, so it is important that you do it with accuracy and quickly. You should be able to type without looking at your keyboard. Practice with tools like Typing.com and measure your speed. An average worker should have at least 45 WPM (Words Per Minute), while a typing specialist can reach 150 WPM. I reach 74 WPM.

Set the mouse speed to maximum. This will help you work faster and reduce wrist strain.

- **Trick** → Search on Windows 'Mouse' or go to 'Devices > Mouse'. Look for 'Select a pointer speed', and drag it all the way to the right to set the speed to 'Fast'.

Create Folders for your Bookmarks. For instance in Chrome:

- Open the options (top-right, 3 vertical points)
- Go to 'Bookmarks and lists > Show bookmarks bar'
- Right-click on that new space, select 'Add folder...' and rename it to 'Jobs'.

Place there the sites that will help you in your searching.

- **Trick** → You can open all of them by right-clicking in the folder and pushing 'Open all', or pushing 'Ctrl' and left-clicking.

Want more tips? For detailed strategies on productivity and organization, check out my book on Amazon: 'How to win time and improve your quality of life. Productivity and organization tricks to enjoy more your day to day'.

3.- Invest your first hour of the day in job searching

Your most important task now is to job searching. Consider waking up at 5 am, when no one will bother you, to start your computer and begin your job search. That means you should go to bed at 10 pm at the latest (at least 7 hours of sleep).

Prioritize important tasks over urgent ones. Well-organized rarely face urgent situations, because they anticipate tasks and potential risks. They organize their schedule to prioritize essential tasks, which are the assignments that will benefit them in the future. And after that, the day-to-day tasks.

Update your knowledge daily. It is relevant to upgrade your skills (hard and soft), as well as being informed of the news of your field, so you know current trends in your field. Also, listen to podcasts and watch videos while working.

4.- Consider working for lower-skilled positions as an investment for the future

I worked for a multinational company, earning 0 euros per month. I could manage for a few months because my parents paid my rent, although I strongly disagreed with it. For me, unpaid or poorly paid internships are an example of exploitation in the 21st century. But I had no other option! However, it improved my CV by letting me add the name of a well-known company in my field.

A Brazilian friend came to Luxembourg as a refugee. He was living in an asylum seeker center, alongside others in similar circumstances. After some weeks, he was able to find a well-paid job in a worldwide company (he is fluent in English and an excellent salesperson).

Sometimes, you may need to work in challenging conditions to gain experience. It's not ideal, but it's an investment in your future. Also, think about working abroad because employers highly value international experience.

SKILLS

5.- Learn languages

Learning languages is the best investment in knowledge. No one tells you that languages are one of the most important parts of a CV, but the more languages you know, the more people you are going to interact with, and the more job offers you can apply for.

If you want a qualified job, you must speak the language used by the company. My first job was at an Ibis Hotel in Luton. The manager told me that my English was OK but not great, so my work was limited to taking dirty dishes and placing them in the dishwasher. If I had a better command of English, I might have been able to work as a waiter.

I met an American in Moscow. I asked him what he was doing in Russia. He explained to me that he was an English teacher, and thanks to this, he could work anywhere.

Which languages are the most powerful? It depends on the city where you want to live, not the country, because some countries like Switzerland speak several languages, but it depends on the region (for example, in the south, they speak more Italian). In general, I would recommend these:

1. **English:** undoubtedly the language of the planet Earth. This is a must. If you aren't an English native, you must learn it.

2. **French:** in my opinion the best investment, as my godmother suggested to me. It is the second most important language in the EU (now even more so after Brexit), many powerful countries in Europe use it, Canada also, it is the official language of some African ex colonies, and it is spoken by many people in Arab countries.

Other options? If you already know English and French, consider learning Spanish, German, Arabic, Chinese, Japanese, Russian, Hindi or Portuguese. Because technology changes, but languages remain.

6.- Learn industry-relevant programs

Focus on widely used programs. There are thousands of programs that are updated daily. It's beneficial to learn the most significant program in each category, rather than trying to master every program, since their features are often similar and widely recognized. For instance:

- **Adobe Illustrator:** Graphic Vector Design
- **Adobe Premiere Pro:** Video Editing
- **Asana:** Project Management
- **Audacity:** Audio Editing
- **Autodesk Maya:** 3D Modelling and Animation
- **ChatGPT:** Conversational AI and Language Model
- **Google Ads:** Online Advertising Platform
- **Google Analytics:** Web and Data Analysis
- **Google Drive:** Cloud Storage
- **Hootsuite:** Social Media Management
- **Mailchimp:** Email Campaign Creation
- **Microsoft 365:** Office Productivity
- **Moodle:** Learning Management Systems (LMS)
- **MySQL:** Database Management Systems
- **Photoshop:** Graphic Design
- **Salesforce:** Customer Relationship Management (CRM)
- **Shopify:** E-commerce Platforms
- **Slack:** Collaboration
- **Tableau:** Data Analysis and Visualization
- **Unity:** Game Development Engines
- **Visual Studio:** Programming and Development Environments
- **WordPress:** Content Management Systems (CMS)

7.- Learn keyboard shortcuts for efficiency

Learn keyboard shortcuts. When working with software, you repeat the same proceedings, and sometimes it's faster to use a keyboard shortcut rather than navigating through menus. Look for shortcuts on the web or in the tool itself, and also in blogs and videos.

NETWORKING

8.- Inform all your contacts about your career goals

You never know who might be able to help, so tell everyone you're looking for a job. Family, friends, WhatsApp groups, Facebook... Tell them what you're looking for, as they may offer advice or connect you with someone else.

The nicer you are and the better your work, the more help you'll receive. I was once at an unemployment office when I met a former colleague. We were both job hunting and talked about our search. A few weeks later, one of her friends called me in the evening. She was having an interview the next morning and needed a copywriter to join the team. Since she knew I was unemployed, she asked if I was interested. We had the interview the next day, and were hired.

If you're currently employed, first decide whether you want to hide your intention to switch companies or be open about it. If your company knows you want to leave, they may improve your conditions, or they could get upset and dismiss you. Think carefully about your situation and the potential problems and benefits.

9.- Attend events to expand your network

You can meet interesting people and companies at events. Go to job fairs, technology expos, industry conferences, workshops, hackathons, seminars, and even social gatherings for professionals.

Prepare your business card. Include your name, phone number, email address, LinkedIn profile, and the position you're seeking, along with some key results. This can be the same heading as your LinkedIn profile. You may want to have different cards for each type of job. Insert a QR code that links directly to your LinkedIn profile. Consider adding a picture of you, because people receive many cards and may not remember who is who.

Prepare your elevator speech. This is a short message to describe who you are, which position you're aiming for, and how your experience and skills will help you succeed. You must deliver it in less than 1 minute (speaking at a normal pace), just as if you were introducing yourself during a brief lift ride.

10.- Join or create groups to connect with people

There are many platforms and groups for various activities. Do some research and participate in some of them to connect with new people in your field. You can find them on platforms such as LinkedIn, Telegram, Meetup, and University Alumni Networks.

Create groups to help you grow. Once, I created a group on Telegram for people who wanted to practice German for free, and we had several conversations on Zoom. Later, we even had the chance to meet one of the guys who was from Azerbaijan in Luxembourg.

LINKEDIN

11.- Create a complete profile

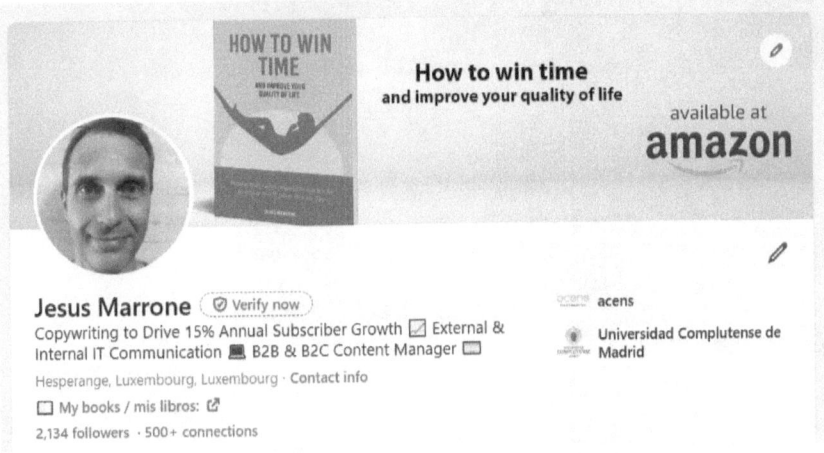

Use a professional-looking photo that presents you well. Smile and wear clothes related to your industry or position.

Take advantage of the background image to engage visitors. It can be an impactful image related to your skills, achievements, or a book you've published.

Make your headline stand out! Your headline is likely the only thing users will read, so make it compelling. You can highlight the following elements:

- Your current position, sector, company, and location
- Skills
- Interests
- Career aspirations
- Results
- Keywords relevant to your field

Adapt your headline to your desired position. If you want to be a salesman, say it, even if you're currently working as a lawyer. Keep in mind that if you send your CV for a sales position but your headline doesn't match, recruiters may rule you out. In the following image, you can see how recruiters search for profiles on LinkedIn.

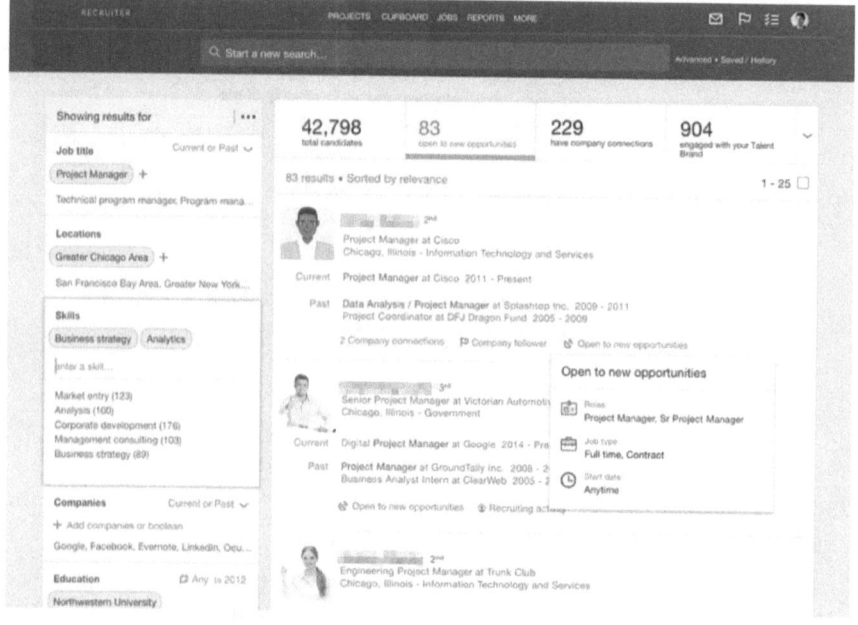

The 'About' section is crucial. The summary can grab the reader's attention, even if you don't think it's important. Explain more about yourself, your goals, your results and what you're looking for.

Personalize your URL to make it more professional. Avoid things like 'johnsmith52941' or 'matbt'. Consider these options:

- **Use your name** (www.linkedin.com/in/jesusmarrone): I think it is the best option. If your name is taken, consider using middle names, initials (real or invented), hyphens, or other generic terms like 'CV' (linkedin.com/in/john-j-smith-cv).

- **You could also include your profession, skills, industry, date of birth, or city** (linkedin.com/in/emilyjones-photography): However, be aware that if you change your location or profession, you'll need to update your URL, which could result in broken links elsewhere (such as in resumes or social media posts).

Add all the languages you know along with your proficiency level. People prefer to talk in their native language, even if the position requires a different one. If a recruiter sees that you're proficient in their native language, they may be more inclined to reach out to you.

12.- Set your profile to #OpenToWork?

There is a debate about whether it's good or not to set #OpenToWork. Some say it benefits the candidate because it lets people know you're available. Others don't recommend it because you may be perceived as desperate for a job. I don't have the answer, but you can try setting it and see if it works for you.

You can set it to be visible only to HR. Once in #OpenToWork, scroll down and select 'Recruiters only', so only people using LinkedIn Recruiter will see you. LinkedIn says that they take steps not to show recruiters at your current company, but they can't guarantee complete privacy.

Visibility (who can view you're open to work)*

○ **Recruiters only**
Limited to people using LinkedIn Recruiter
While we take steps not to show recruiters at your current company, we can't guarantee complete privacy.

○ **All LinkedIn members**
Includes recruiters and people at your current company
This selection adds the #OpenToWork photo frame.

You can set it to 'All LinkedIn members'. This means that recruiters and people at your current company will see the #OpenToWork frame on your profile picture. Who knows, maybe your employer sees it and gets upset, or perhaps they'll offer you a salary raise.

13.- Master the search tools

Search for jobs in a city without specifying a position. Go to LinkedIn:

- Click on the 'Jobs' menu
- Leave the 'Title, skill or company' field empty
- In the location field, enter the name of the city where you want to work and press 'Enter'
- In the 'Remote' drop-down menu, select 'On-site' and 'Hybrid'
- Then click 'Show results'. You will see all the positions that are open in that area!

- **Trick** → I don't recommend clicking 'Remote' because doing so will show offers for the entire country or even the EU. You'll be competing with thousands of people, which greatly reduces your chances of getting the job.

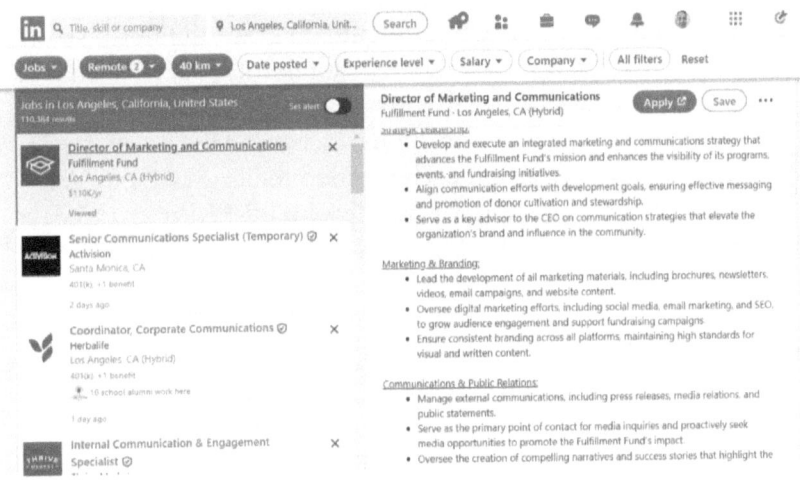

Make the most of the filters:

- Click on 'All filters' at the top right to display all the options to personalize your search
- You can click 'Sort by > Most recent' and 'Dated posted > Past week' to see positions that are likely still open
- You can specify that you want a 'Full-time position' or an 'Internship', and filter for many other factors
- Keep in mind that in the 'Distance' filter, you can set a smaller distance to find positions closer to your location, but you will see fewer offers.
- Remember to click 'Show results' to apply the filters.

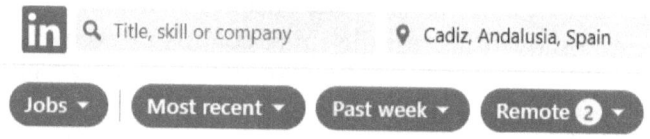

Search for positions with few applicants. Click 'All filters', scroll down and activate the option 'Under 10 applicants'. As you can see, there will be fewer results, but the advantage is that fewer than 10 people have applied for those positions, increasing your chances of getting an interview. Note that each position indicates when it was posted, so it's better to search for positions published at least 5 days ago with fewer than 10 applicants to maximize your chances.

- **Trick →** Scroll down to see a series of numbers at the bottom of the page. Click on the three horizontal dots (...) and repeat this several times until you reach the last page of the search. Now you have reached positions published 6 days ago with fewer than 10 applicants. Go for them!

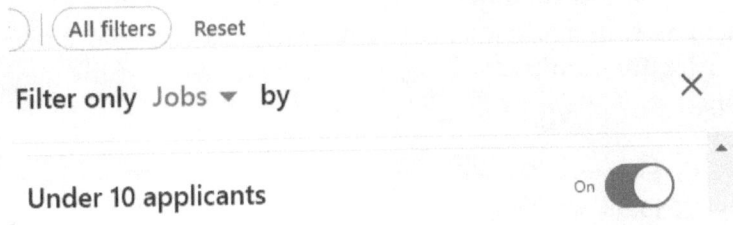

14.- Save your job alerts

After refining a search, click 'Set alert'. This way, LinkedIn will notify you about new opportunities:

- You'll see a pop-up at the bottom of the page that says 'Manage alerts'
- You can also go there by clicking 'Jobs > Preferences > Job alerts'
- You will see all the job searches you have saved, and you can edit them by clicking the pencil icon
- I think that is better to set 'Alert frequency > Daily' and 'Notification type > Email'
- By default, the option 'Get notified of similar jobs when no jobs match your alert' is enabled, but you can disable it if you start receiving too many irrelevant emails

Create several job searches and save them. This process will take time to master, so don't hesitate to make different tests. Since there are many filters, for example, you can save multiple alerts for the same position:

1. UX Designer, On-site
2. UX Designer, Hybrid
3. UX Designer, Remote

Therefore, you will receive 3 emails each day for the same position, but with different job offers, as you have specified various characteristics for each search. This way, you can determine which search is helping you send more CVs and get more interviews.

15.- Search for job postings

LinkedIn is a platform for jobs, networking, and sharing professional information. As you may know, people post information on this social network, including job vacancies! To find them, open 3 new tabs in your web browser, go to LinkedIn in each tab, and in the search bar of each tab, type the following:

- Tab 1: **Hiring** + *[city name]*
- Tab 2: **Great opportunity** + *[city name]*
- Tab 3: **Join** + *[city name]*

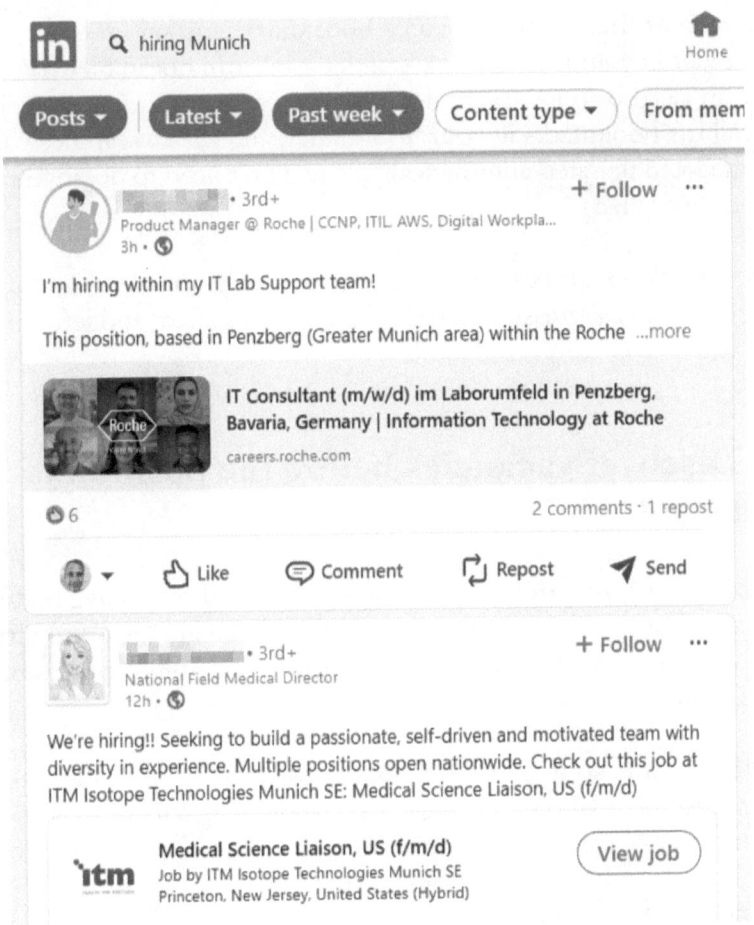

For instance, type 'Hiring Munich', press 'Enter', click 'Posts' and set 'Sort by > Most recent' and 'Date posted > Last week'. Voilà! Now you can see posts that request applicants for job positions that might not be listed in the 'Jobs' section, so you would never have known about them without using this trick.

Save each of these job posts as a bookmark, and save them in your 'Job' folder in your Chrome bookmarks (LinkedIn doesn't let you create an alert for this). Every day when you start your job search, just open all the bookmarks in your 'Job' folder, and all the searches will be refreshed and updated automatically. You won't need to do anything else but find jobs.

- **Trick** → You can open all of them by right-clicking in the folder and pressing 'Open all', or clicking 'Ctrl' and left-clicking.

16.- Discover vacancies before the position is published

The early bird gets the worm! Finding a job is about timing and being the first to act. No one wants to conduct 30 interviews to hire someone, they hope the first candidate is the ideal one. Sometimes, the position might not even be published...

That's why it is so important to network. Meet people online and at events. Tell them who you are, what you're looking for, and ask them to notify you when a relevant position opens. This requires significant effort, but it can be very rewarding. I didn't get any jobs from my close contacts, but I got opportunities through university colleagues, former coworkers, and other connections.

I came up with an idea to find job openings. Before continuing, read the previous section 'Search for job postings' to better follow my idea. If you've already done that, keep reading.

Go to LinkedIn and search 'Starting a new position + *[city name]*:

- Then press 'Post'
- Set 'Sort by > Most recent'
- Set Date posted > Past 24 hours'

This will show you a list of people who have recently announced new jobs. Their previous positions may still be open!

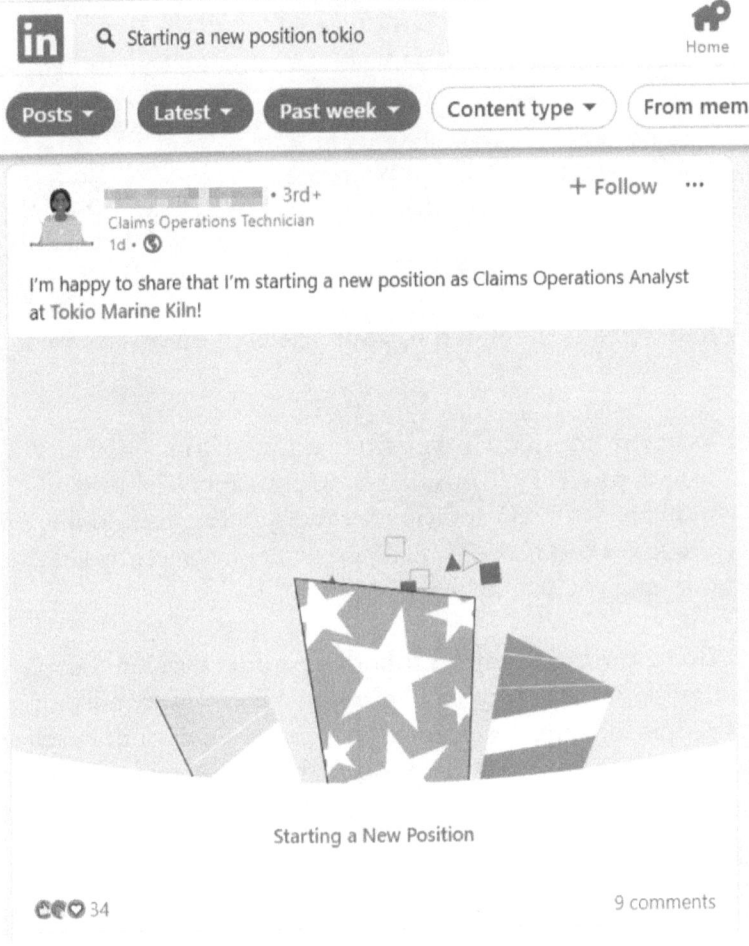

Go to the person's profile and check their Experience section, to see their most recent position and company.

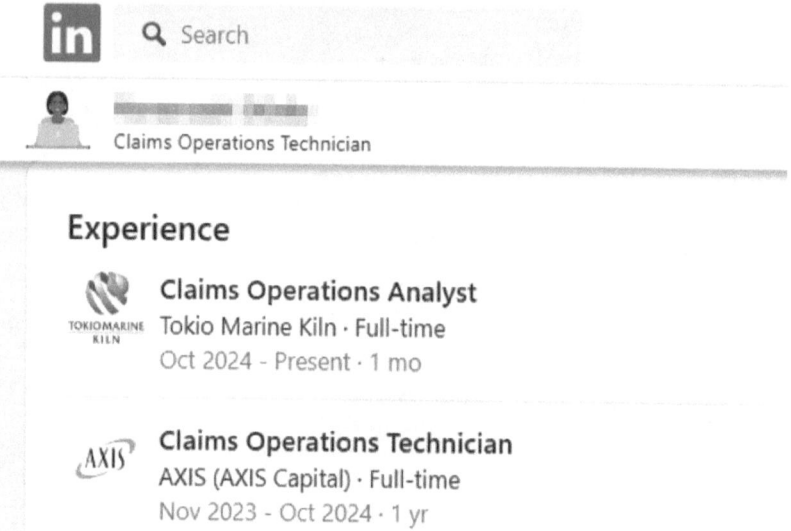

If they had a position related to your search, you can do two things:

- **Visit the company's website:** go to the 'Jobs / Careers' section to see if the position is open to apply, or send a spontaneous email applying for the position, mentioning that you know John Doe (a made-up name) has recently left the role, and you would like to apply for it.

- **Go to the company's LinkedIn profile:** click on 'People', and use the search bar to type 'recruiter'. You will see a list of people in Human Resources or Talent Acquisition. Reach out to them to apply for the position (having mutual connections can increase your chances of getting a response).

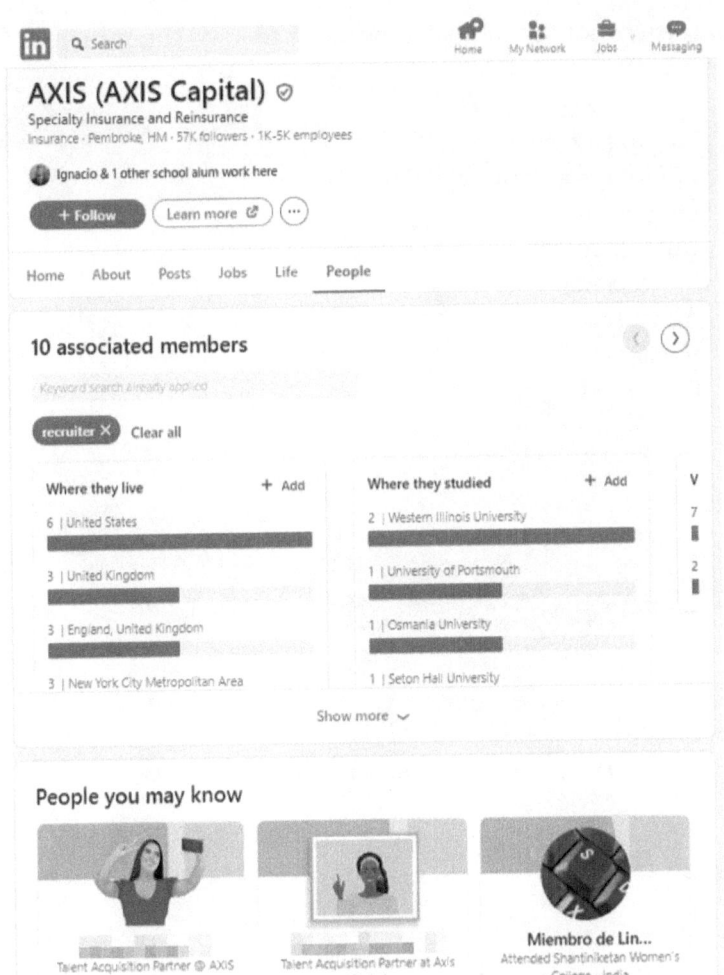

You can try other searches (remember to save them in your 'Jobs' folder in Chrome):

- Seeking a new role
- Looking for new opportunities
- Urgent hire
- Immediate start
- Job seeking
- Actively looking
- Vacancy
- Promoted
- *[Write desired position]*

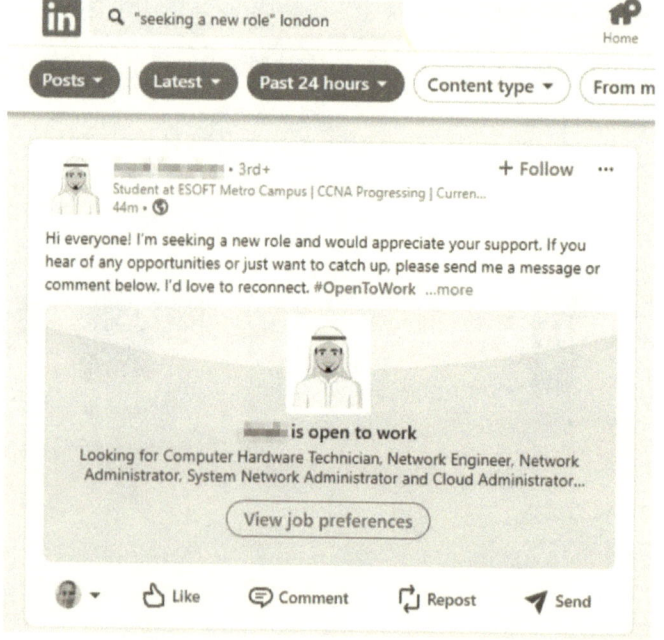

17.- Connect with people and network

Add people on LinkedIn, even if you don't know them. This can lead to new opportunities, and it could also be beneficial when a recruiter sees that you have mutual connections. Additionally, you will receive their updates in your feed. Add people working in the same field as you who are based in the city where you want to live. The more people you add, the better.

Contact recruiters. You can connect with them and send your CV along with your expectations. Additionally, share what you're struggling with. Maybe they can help you.

Ask people for information. You can message them something like:

"I'm reaching out because I've seen that you have a strong career path and experience in [write position].

I'm currently exploring job opportunities in that area and would love to get your insights on effective job search strategies".

You can suggest having a 10-minute call and maybe ask them about opportunities at their company (in this case, it's better to contact someone in a different department than the one you're interested in).

Ask if they see any opportunities at their company. If you have a mutual connection, LinkedIn will show you in the 'People you can reach out to' section. You can ask them about the environment is like and the possibilities for growth, for instance. Or ask for tips for the interview!

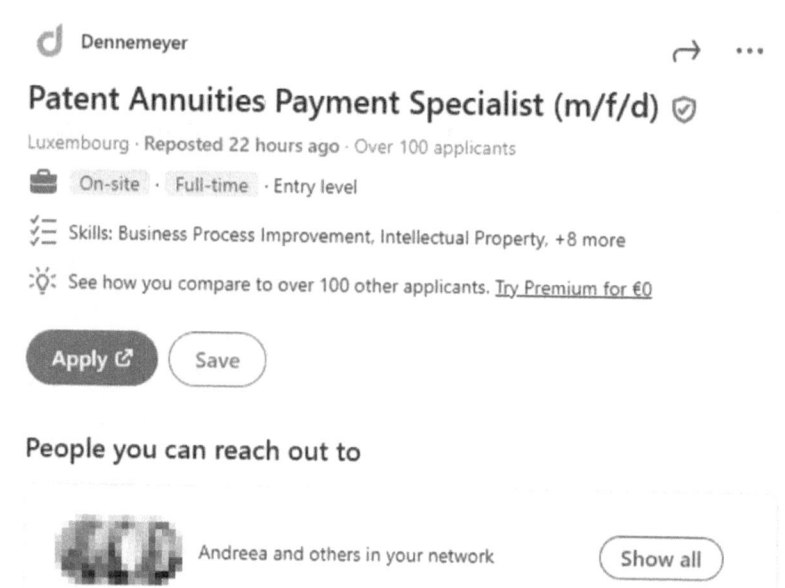

18.- Ask for referrals

After applying for a position, look for people who can help you. It can be mutual connections (as explained before).

- Check the LinkedIn profile of the company
- Click 'People'
- Push the right arrow until you reach 'How you're connected'
- See if you have a 1st-degree connection.
- If not, click on 2nd-degree connection when available (someone who is a mutual contact between you and them)
- Scroll down and choose someone to contact.

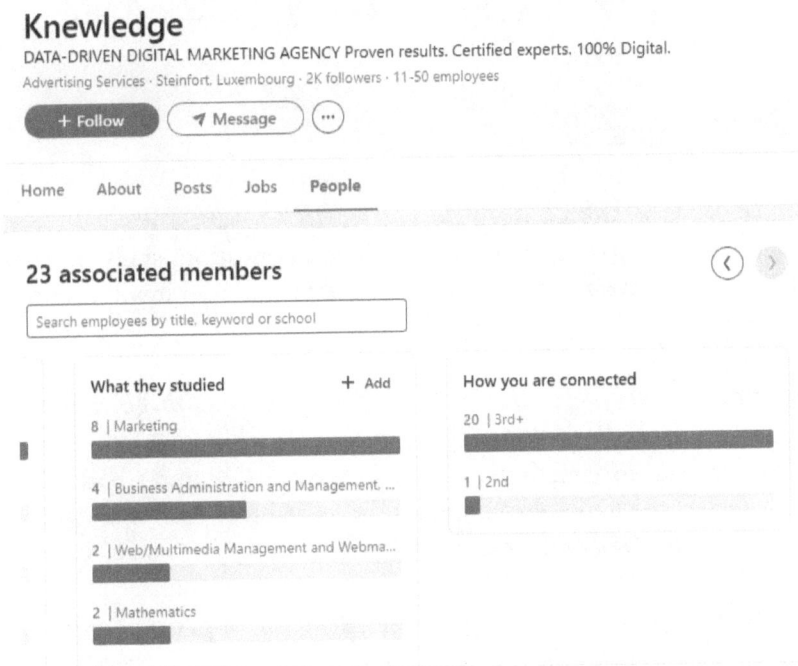

Send them a private message, like this (adapted from the book 'Career Coach GPT', by Jeremy Schifeling):

"Hi [name], I'm very interested in the [position] role at [company] and would be grateful if you'd consider referring me :)

Here's my resume: [link to your LinkedIn profile]

I hope you get a great referral bonus from it!".

Referrals take you 10 steps ahead of other candidates. HR manages hundreds of CVs, so when a colleague refers a candidate, the recruiter is much more likely to take interest.

CHATGPT

19.- CV ideas

"Create my CV, which data do you need?". ChatGPT will ask for your personal information, work experience, education, skills, language proficiency, achievements, etc. Provide the details, and it will create your CV.

"These are my skills [paste skills], which positions might I would be a good fit for? Please justify". You can also add your experience. Provide all your information, or even paste your CV, and ChatGPT will give you ideas for new jobs you might be suited for. Also ask: *"Are there other positions unrelated to this that I could pivot to?"*.

"This is my CV [paste CV], give me ideas for improvement". Copy and paste your resume or even upload it, then use that prompt (instruction) so ChatGPT can suggest ways to refine its structure, clarity, and impact. Then start modifying your CV (make a backup first) and ask ChatGPT for feedback on each section (as if you were talking with a professional coach). Once you finish, upload it again and ask: *"Rate my CV from 0-10"*.

> **CV Rating: 9/10**
>
> Your CV is excellent and demonstrates your expertise, achievements, and relevance for a Communications Specialist role effectively. Here's the breakdown:
>
> **Strengths:**
>
> 1. **Clear Objective and Branding:**
>   - The opening statement is concise and impactful, showcasing key achievements like increasing subscribers and customer satisfaction metrics.
>   - Phrases like "Translating complexity into simplicity" are memorable and align well with a Communications Specialist role.
>
> 2. **Achievements-Oriented:**

"Here is my CV [paste CV], create a new one tailored for the position of Project Manager". With this prompt, ChatGPT will generate a new resume, emphasizing the information related to the position. You can try this with any jobs you like. Remember that you should review and refine the content generated by the AI.

"This is the job offer [paste job offer], tailor my CV to match this position [paste CV]". ChatGPT will highlight the relevant skills, experiences, and achievements that best align with the position. It's a kind of magic!

"Add my experience with Photoshop and remove the mention of my knowledge of Markdown". You can revise the CV and sections, requesting ChatGPT to make changes. However, keep in mind that generative AI can sometimes 'hallucinate' (i.e., provide incorrect information), so ask it to remove specific details and check for misspellings and grammar errors. For example, say: *"Review my text for mistakes and suggest corrections"*, or simply, *"Mistakes"*.

"Provide prompts to help me improve my CV". You will receive suggestions that will enhance your resume. Keep in mind that companies use Applicant Tracking Systems (ATS), software that scans resumes for relevant skills and qualifications that match job requirements. Using the right keywords increases your chances of standing out on ATS and getting noticed by recruiters.

- **Trick** → If you're on the free plan and exceed the usage limit, you can close the window and open a new ChatGPT session to regain normal access. Alternatively, you can create another account using a different email to continue using the service.

20.- Cover letter creation

Recruiters may not always read cover letters, but they value candidates who include them. You should include your letter of

motivation, but don't spend too much time on it.
"This is the job offer [paste job offer], this is my CV [paste CV], create a cover letter". ChatGPT will generate a cover letter that fits the position, based on your CV. This is the way.

"Make it shorter". Typically, generative AI tends to produce lengthy content with long paragraphs. A cover letter should tell your details in three short paragraphs: one covering the position, one about the company, and one discussing your relevant skills, experience, and motivations. If it's concise, they will read it. Highlight one key sentence per paragraph using bold text.

21.- Interview practice

"This is the job offer [paste job offer], this is my CV [paste CV], act as the recruiter and ask me interview questions, then provide answers". ChatGPT will generate questions along with appropriate answers. You can ask: *"Give me more"*, and it will provide additional ones.

"For the question 'Why do you think you'd be a good fit for this role', this is my answer [paste answer]. Improve it". This prompt will help make your answer clearer, more tailored to the job description, and more compelling to recruiters.

"How can I ask them about salary / holidays / telework... ?". Feel free to ask ChatGPT for assistance in crafting a polite question to gather more information about the offer's terms.

- Trick → **Practice pronunciation and listening with Gemini.** This generative AI from Google has a built-in microphone, available both in the app and in the browser. You can converse with it in any language! It's great for practising interviews, either by using the same prompts as before or by saying: *"Let's make a dialogue. You are the recruiter for this position [say job position], interview me"*.

22.- Salary research

"This is the job offer [paste job offer], this is the enterprise [web link]. What is the likely salary range?". ChatGPT will give you an estimation based on the job position, the enterprise and the location.

"Give me negotiation tips". It can offer advice on how to approach salary negotiations based on industry standards and your level of experience. Don't forget that there are other benefits, such as holidays, remote work, private health insurance, or professional development opportunities.

23.- Job Search Assistance

Press the 'Search the web' button. ChatGPT will search the web to provide up-to-date information.

"Find [position] jobs in [location]". For instance: *"Find Software Developer jobs in Tokyo"*.

WEBSITES

24.- Create alerts on Google

Visit Alerts (www.google.com/alerts) and customize your search to automatically receive updates. Enter keywords related to the position or information you'd like to track, and Google will send the latest news to your email.

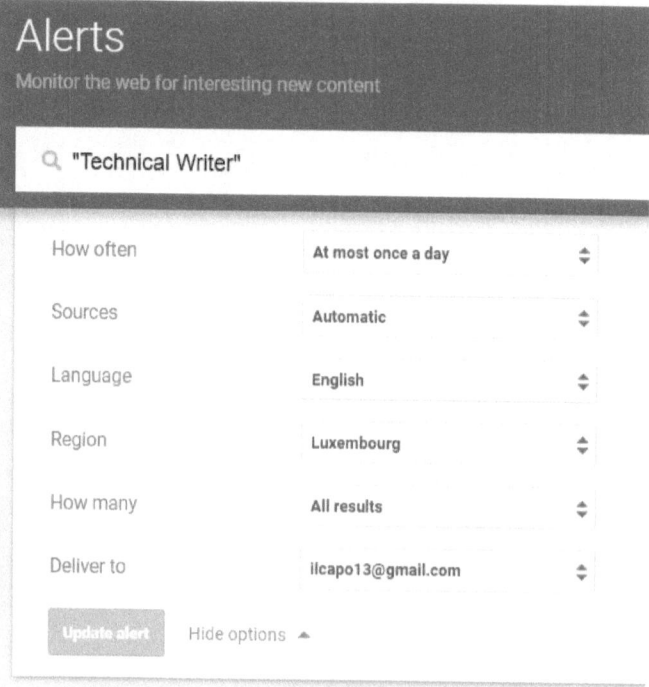

25.- Search for companies, recruiters and job boards

Indeed, Glassdoor, and CareerBuilder can send you new job postings, just like LinkedIn. Also, check the careers sections of company websites, which may include job listings and even offer email alerts for new postings. Don't forget to reach out to recruiters about future opportunities. You may also consider contacting headhunters or the employment office for assistance.

26.- Spontaneous applications

Create a list of companies and their email addresses. Send them your CV and express your interest in potential opportunities.

27.- Search in different languages

Search for positions in the languages you speak. This way, you will multiply the chances of finding a job. My wife was living in Madrid and searched for jobs in German, knowing that there would be less competition. Thanks to this strategy, she was able to find a job.

CV

28.- Highlight the city, position, experience, results, skills and languages

At the top, include your personal information and the city of the job offer. Having the same location as the job offer increases your chances of getting an interview, where you can explain that, although you are not currently living there, you are willing to relocate (make sure you know beforehand if you need a work visa).

Highlight the position and the company you're applying to. This will help you stand out in Applicant Tracking Systems (ATS). Since recruiters manage thousands of CVs, they'll easily see which position you're seeking. Use a larger font size so it's clear at first glance. For example: *"I am applying for the position of Compliance Officer (Mitsubishi)"*.

The most important thing in a CV is the experience. It's the first thing recruiters look for, and they are particularly interested if you've worked at well-known companies or in relevant countries. Don't include everything you've done to avoid making it too long, focus on the most relevant experiences. A quick example:

Compliance Officer at IBM

Tokyo, Japan (2020 - Present)

- **Responsibilities**: Oversee compliance with regulatory requirements, conduct risk assessments, ensure company policies align with legal standards.
- **Key Results**: Reduced compliance-related fines by 15% through proactive risk management and staff training.
- **Skills**: Regulatory compliance, risk assessment, legal research, project management, communication.
- **Computer skills**: Microsoft Office 365, MetricStream and Tableau.

Include only relevant experience for the specific position. If you were a Cook, that experience may not be helpful when applying for a Customer Service role (skip it). However, if you were a Chef, you can mention how you learned to organize people in stressful situations.

Avoid including months in the dates unless you held several positions during the same year. This will help you to not spotlight gaps in your career. See the difference, I prefer Option B, and you?

Option A:
- July 2021 - October 2022 **Google**
- March 2023 - September 2024 **Netflix**

Option B:
- 2021 - 2022 **Google**
- 2023 - 2024 **Netflix**

Explain employment gaps. If you have a significant professional gap, whether due to unemployment or working in a field unrelated to your target role, you will need to explain it. If you don't, people will notice and they will mistrust you. If you were working on a personal project, treat it like any other job and describe it in the same way. If not, you can say:

- *"I took time off to care for a family member"*
- *"I focused on freelance work"*, *"I learnt Japanese to reach that market"*
- *"I completed a certification course in AWS"*
- *"I spent a year travelling, which allowed me to broaden my cultural awareness and language skills, enhancing my ability to work in diverse international teams"*.

Example:

- 2020 - 2021 **Employment Gap:** took time off to finalize and submit my thesis for Journalism. During this time, I focused on writing, analysis, and completing my academic project, further developing my skills in **copywriting, investigative research, and networking**.

Education and soft skills usually only matter for your first job. If you are a university graduate you won't have many experience, so focus on your degree, proactive attitudes and willing to learn. When you are a Senior, maybe they value more specific trainings for your upskilling.

1 or 2 pages is ideal. Recruiters typically spend around 10 seconds scanning your CV, so avoid overcrowding it with text. Instead, summarize and simplify, creating a document that is easy and pleasant to read. If you worked in many places, group them: *"(2002 - 2008) Creative Copywriter at Bassat-Ogilvy and other advertising agencies"*.

29.- One CV for each position

Tailor your CV for each position. If you are applying for Spanish teacher and Spanish translator, both CV can't be exactly the same, you must have 2 CV.

The ideal approach is to have a CV ready to send. This means you can send the PDF without modifying anything. This has the advantage that you can apply in seconds, but on the other hand you can forget to write the exact position and the company you are applying for. To solve this, you can have 2 versions of your CV:

- **Ready to send:** for jobs you're not very interested in or jobs you think you don't have much chance at, you can quickly send this PDF.

- **Template:** a Word file in which you need to modify it for each job offer: *"I am applying for the position of [position] ([enterprise])"*. For example: *"I am applying for the position of IP Specialist (Dennemeyer)"*.

30.- Rename your CV file to include your name and the position

Tailor the file name to the position you are applying for. A recruiter should be able to know your name and position without opening the file, making their job easier. See the difference?

1. cv_final_version

2. CV Communications Specialist (Jesus Marrone)

You can add the company name, but it will take more time. Job hunting takes a lot of energy, so try to minimize the effort involved in sending each CV. This will help you stay motivated to send out more applications.

INTERVIEWS

31.- Increase your chances of landing interviews

On average, you need to be involved in 6 hiring processes to get 1 job. Recruiters interview 4-6 candidates for a position, which means that when they call you for an interview, you have a 25%-16% chance of getting the job. So, if you enter 6 job processes, you're likely to get a job.

These were my statistics for finding a job in Luxembourg. As you can see, the more CVs I sent, the more interviews I had:

- **2023:**
    - 62 CVs sent
    - 2 hiring processes

- **2024:**
    - 245 CVs sent
    - 6 hiring processes

The more CVs you send, the more interviews you get. Assuming you need to send 40 CVs to get shortlisted and start a hiring process, in general, you have to send around 240 CVs to get a job.

You need to generate many interviews to increase your chances. One way to do this is by applying to different positions, even if you're not particularly interested, because it will help you improve your odds and enhance your performance during interviews.

32.- Word document for interview plan

Create a Word template with all the information needed for an interview. Hiring processes are similar, and they usually ask the same questions, so it's helpful to have notes to guide your responses. Don't forget to save the link to the offer, and it's better to download it to have a copy in case they delete it.

Document information about the company. Search the web and Google to gather this data, so you know more about what the company does and how you can contribute to its growth.

The recruiter is your key to the job. Making a good impression increases your chances of getting the position. Visit the recruiter's LinkedIn profile and search for their information on Google to learn about their career, skills, languages, hobbies, and the places they've lived. There may be common ground or shared interests, which could work in your favour.

Prepare your introductory pitch tailored to the position and company. They will always ask about your career, so summarize your education (related to the position), key companies you've worked for, your skills, results, languages (if applicable), and how you can contribute to the company. You can finish your pitch with a question, such as the one in the following paragraph.

Ask the interviewer about your CV. According to the renowned psychologist Robert B. Cialdini in his book 'Influence: The Psychology of Persuasion', try asking: *"What part of my resume caught your attention to make me a candidate?"*. This question encourages the interviewer to focus on your strengths, boosting your chances of getting hired.

If you are unemployed, they will ask you about your previous job. If you left it to pursue another project, explain it. Did they fire you? Then consider giving a simple and neutral response, such as: *"There was a company restructuring"*. Avoid speaking negatively about previous employers.

If you are currently employed, the interviewer will ask why you want to change jobs. While seeking better pay and conditions is common, it's more strategic to say that you're looking to grow in your career. In my case, it was simple: my wife was working in Luxembourg, so I needed a job there (and the company values family stability). For example, you might explain that you're interested in:

- *"Gaining more experience in a different field"*
- *"Looking to contribute to more strategic projects"*
- *"Taking on more leadership responsibilities"*
- *"Seeking long-term growth opportunities"*
- *"Excited to learn new skills"*
- *"Searching for a company with a culture that aligns better with my values"*

They will often ask about your salary expectations. To prepare, research the job, company, and country on sites like Google, Indeed, and Glassdoor. You can also ask ChatGPT for help. Another option is to counter-ask them: *"Could you tell me the salary range for this position?"*. I've tried this three times: it worked once, and in the other two cases, they said they couldn't share it, but they didn't get upset. I just gave them my numbers.

There are two situations to think about:

- **If you need a job quickly:** ask for a salary lower than the average to improve your chances. But don't ask for too little, as it might make you seem unprepared.

- **If you're not in a rush:** you can ask for a higher salary than average. This shows confidence in your skills. If they don't hire you, it's fine because you're not in a hurry.

If you're employed, you must know your notice period. This may be in your contract; if not, check for the information so you can know exactly how many weeks you need to stay in your job before leaving. Sometimes, the notice period depends on the day of the month you resign, so make sure to calculate it carefully. If you're unsure, consider speaking with the Employee Committee or Human Resources. Keep in mind, however, that the company may suspect you're planning to leave. If your notice period is only 2 weeks, it can be a good gesture to offer 4 weeks, giving your current company more time to find a replacement

Don't forget to answer like this: *"X weeks/months after signing the contract"*. Hiring processes can take a long time, and you're not sure you'll get the job until you sign the contract. So, it's important to be clear about this during the interview.

Other common recruiter's questions:

- How do you handle conflicts at work?
- Can you give an example of a task you struggled with?
- Can you give an example of a task you delivered successfully?
- How do you collaborate with colleagues and manage your workload?
- What can you contribute to our company?
- How would your manager describe you?
- What are your 3 main strengths/weaknesses?

You can ask about this information:

- Is this a permanent position?
- Is this position office-based or hybrid?
- What are the working hours?
- What kind of projects would I be working on (e.g., apps, websites, platforms)?
- Could you tell me about the bonus package?
- Could you explain how many stages are involved in the hiring process?
- If you could design the ideal candidate for this position, what skills and traits would they possess?
- What do you see as the biggest challenges facing your company in the next six months?

33.- Before the interview

Be mindful of the time zone when scheduling the interview. The interviewer could be in another country, or even within the same country, they may be in a different time zone (for example, you live in New York and they live in Los Angeles). Also, try to schedule it at a time when there is less noise at your home.

Confirm the application you'll use for the interview. If they don't tell you, ask to test that you can access it properly (with a friend or even by yourself using two computers or your mobile). Also, have backup options in case of technical issues, such as suggesting a WhatsApp video call as a last resort.

Prepare your devices. Make sure your phone and laptop batteries are fully charged (plugged in if possible and connected to the router via Ethernet cable). If the power goes out where you are, you can continue the interview by activating your phone's Wi-Fi hotspot and connecting to it from your computer (using mobile data).

Have a bright and appropriate background. It's important that the interviewer can see you clearly, with good lighting, and that your background looks professional. You can use simple virtual backgrounds, such as a plain-coloured wall or a bookshelf with perfectly arranged books.

Practice and record yourself. It's helpful to see how you express yourself and move, so you can get comfortable. If possible, share it with someone to get their honest feedback.

Make ChatGPT ask you tough questions. In addition to researching the company interviewing you and trying out their services, if possible, you can simulate an interview with ChatGPT (see the chapter in this book), which will ask you questions based on your responses.

34.- During the interview

Dress as if the interview were in person. Wear the appropriate attire for the position, including the right shoes, as the interviewer may ask you to stand. This will also help you mentally prepare for the situation.

Conduct the interview in a quiet room. Close doors and windows to block out external noise, and turn off any devices that make distracting sounds (such as the washing machine or dishwasher). Avoid other distractions, such as phone notifications.

Use headphones with a microphone. This will allow you to hear the other person more clearly and vice versa (it's not recommended to use the laptop's built-in microphone). Speak a bit louder than usual and slowly, so you are understood clearly.

Log in 10 minutes before the scheduled time. This helps avoid last-minute stress. Simply open the app and wait for the other person to connect. If something goes wrong, you'll have time to restart your computer and try again, or be prepared to connect with your phone or tablet.

Look at the camera and be mindful of your posture. If you're using a portable camera, place it above the screen. It's not ideal if the interviewer sees you from the side. Make sure your head is at the top of the frame and that your chest is visible. Your posture and body language should show confidence and professionalism.

Keep your Word document for the interview plan nearby. You can place it on another part of the screen, on a second monitor, or on paper that's not visible, along with a copy of your CV. Don't hesitate to ask questions about the company and jot down key details the interviewer shares. This shows that you've done your research and are genuinely interested in the job. At the end of the interview, thank them for the opportunity and express your readiness for the position.

35.- After the interview

Follow-up the interview. It's a good idea to send an email after the interview to reiterate your interest in the position. It's generally best to send it in the afternoon (around 14:00, depending on the country), as people are usually less busy and happier after lunch. Additionally, avoid sending it on a Friday, as the recruiter may forget after the weekend.

Here's an example of what you can say (you may also include a link to any relevant information discussed):

"Dear Hiring team,

Thank you for taking the time to interview me for the position of [position], at [company name].

I enjoyed learning more about the team, and I am even more enthusiastic about the opportunity to contribute to [specific aspect of the job or company discussed].

I look forward to the opportunity of working together.

Best regards,
[Your name]"

Provide feedback to the hiring company. If you are hired by a company but will be working for another (such as in a consulting or outsourced role), it's important to keep the hiring company informed. Send them regular updates on your progress, any challenges faced, and successes achieved. This demonstrates professionalism and helps maintain a positive relationship with your hiring company, even if you're not working directly under them.

Don't expect everyone to respond to you. We've all experienced situations where you have an interview, and the recruiters don't get back to you. This happens everywhere. You can try following up by sending an email or calling, but after the third attempt, don't waste any more time on it. If they don't respond, assume that you were not selected.

What should you do when you receive an email saying you have not been selected? I usually don't reply because the email often comes from a do-not-reply account, and since I've been rejected, I prefer not to waste time. However, you can reply with something like: *"Thank you for letting me know. I am available for future opportunities"*. You might also consider trying to convince them that they've made a mistake. I've read that this approach works occasionally, so you can try it if you think it's worth the effort.

ORGANIZE YOUR JOB SEARCH MATERIALS ONLINE

36.- Save all your job-search materials

Use an online platform to save your materials. It could be Google Drive, Microsoft Office 365... the key is to have access from all your devices at any time, so you can easily edit and update them.

Organize your files into folders, so when a company contacts you, you're ready to provide everything they need. Create separate folders for each language in which you're applying. Here are some suggestions:

- Applications
- Certifications
- Cover letter
- CV
- Interviews
- Picture
- Portfolio
- Referrals

37.- Keep a record of all your applications

Save your applications in a single Word document. Include the position, company, job offer link, and salary (if requested). This will allow you to quickly access the offer if the employer contacts you, and help you check if you've already applied for a particular job.

ACKNOWLEDGMENTS

To my wife for encouraging me during the moments I wanted to give up and stop job hunting, suggesting that I look for other related positions to increase my chances. This motivated me to keep going, and I was able to do a few interviews to practice. ☺

Many thanks to my father for reviewing this work, to my friend Luis Carneiro for the beautiful cover design, and to my psychologist Vicente Crespo for his advice.

For any comments, corrections, suggestions, or inquiries about my services, feel free to contact me at:
content@jesusmarrone.com

You can also connect with me on LinkedIn:
www.linkedin.com/in/jesusmarrone/

I would appreciate it if you could rate this book on Amazon, using a scale from 1 star (very poor) to 5 stars (excellent). This helps others quickly decide whether it's worth reading. Please send me a screenshot (it may take a few days for the rating to appear), and I'd be happy to send you my template for the 'Interview Plan' Word document.

www.ingramcontent.com/pod-product-compliance
Lightning Source LLC
Chambersburg PA
CBHW031550210526
45464CB00003B/1237